HOW DID TEA AND TAXES SPARK A REVOLUTION?

And Other Questions about the Boston Tea Party

Linda Gondosch

LERNER PUBLICATIONS COMPANY · MINNEAPOLIS

A Word about Language

English word usage, spelling, grammar, and punctuation have changed over the centuries. We have preserved original spellings and word usage in the quotations included in this book.

Lerner Publications Company
A division of Lerner Publishing Group, Inc.
241 First Avenue North
Minneapolis, MN 55401 U.S.A.

Website address: www.lernerbooks.com

Library of Congress Cataloging-in-Publication Data

Gondosch, Linda.
    How did tea and taxes spark a revolution? And other questions about the
Boston Tea Party / by Linda Gondosch.
        p.   cm. — (Six questions of American history)
    Includes bibliographical references and index.
    ISBN 978–1–58013–666–2 (lib. bdg. : alk. paper)
    1. Boston Tea Party, 1773—Juvenile literature. I. Title.
E215.7.G66 2011
973.3'115—dc22   2009047329

Manufactured in the United States of America
1 – DP – 7/15/10

TABLE OF CONTENTS

THE SIX QUESTIONS HELP YOU DISCOVER THE FACTS!

INTRODUCTION

SPLASH! One December night in 1773, a wooden chest dropped into the moonlit water of Boston Harbor in Massachusetts. More than one hundred men, many disguised as Native Americans, worked quickly and quietly on board three ships. They hauled up 342 chests filled with tea leaves to the top deck and slashed them open with their axes. They dumped the precious tea overboard into the water and heaved the empty chests in after.

Hundreds of townsfolk watched from the dock and shoreline. Two warships with loaded guns were nearby. British soldiers could attack at any minute. There was no time to talk. The "Indians" knew the destruction of the tea had to be finished by midnight—not one minute later.

Destroying the tea was against the law. The men were defying King George III of Great Britain. They could be tried for a crime against the government, thrown into jail, and hanged. Why would they risk their lives just to destroy a cargo of tea? Why would they anger King George III?

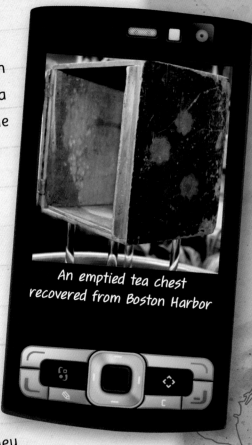

An emptied tea chest recovered from Boston Harbor

NEW
HAMPSHIRE

MASSACHUSETTS
BOSTON

NEW
YORK

RHODE
ISLAND

CONNECTICUT

PENNSYLVANIA

NEW
JERSEY

DELAWARE

MARYLAND

BRITISH

TERRITORY

VIRGINIA

NORTH
CAROLINA

ATLANTIC
OCEAN

SOUTH
CAROLINA

GEORGIA

THE ORIGINAL
THIRTEEN
COLONIES

GULF
OF
MEXICO

Colonists, dressed as Native Americans, throw tea into Boston Harbor in 1773. This print was made in 1789.

WHO
WHAT
WHERE
WHY
WHEN
HOW
WHO
WHAT
WHERE
WHY
WHEN

WHERE
WHY
WHEN
HOW

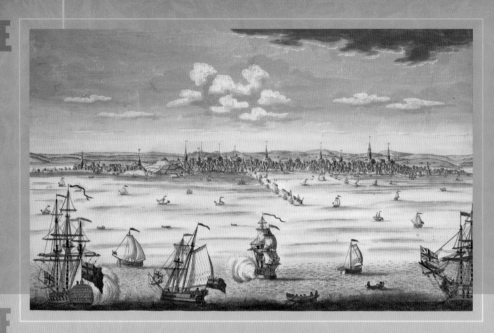

This print by William Burgis shows a busy Boston Harbor in the early 1700s.

ONE NO TAXATION WITHOUT REPRESENTATION

territories settled by people away from their home country. The home country rules the colony.

For years King George III had taxed the colonies in North America to raise money for Great Britain. The colonists had to obey the tax laws even though they had no say in making them. They had no representatives (people who spoke for them) in the British government. "Unfair!" the colonists cried. Why should they obey laws made in Britain? "No taxation without representation!" they argued.

When ships arrived in Boston carrying tea in 1773, import duties (taxes on goods brought into a country) had to be paid on the cargo. But a shocking thing happened. The colonists said "No!" They'd had enough of King George and his taxes. It was time to stand up for their rights. They would show the king they would no longer obey laws made without their consent. To avoid paying the tea tax, they dumped the tea into Boston Harbor.

That December night was a turning point in history. To understand what triggered the rebellion, let's turn back the clock.

Britain first built permanent colonies in North America in the early 1600s. Britain

King George III of Great Britain

ruled these faraway territories. But for more than one hundred years, the colonies had mostly been left alone. The British government passed tax laws to control trade, but the laws were not enforced. The American colonists grew used to taking care of themselves. They ran their own schools and churches. They made their own laws. They enjoyed their freedom.

In 1754 the French and Indian War broke out in the colonies. British, French, and Native Americans fought one another over control of North America. The war ended in 1763. But the war caused important changes in the colonies.

The war had left Great Britain with a huge debt (money owed). Also, Britain saw that it needed an army in the colonies to defend British land. King George decided to tax the colonists again. This time the laws would be strictly enforced. After all, he thought, shouldn't the colonists help pay off Britain's debts and pay for an army?

Parliament passed the Sugar Act in 1764. Colonists would have to pay import duties on sugar and molasses shipped into the colonies. Samuel Adams, a popular political leader in Boston, protested. He wrote, "If taxes are laid upon us . . . without our having a legal Representation . . . are we not reduced from . . . free Subjects to the miserable State of . . . Slaves?" Adams's fiery words were printed in several newspapers.

Many colonists agreed with Adams. They did not want Parliament making laws for them. Besides, they

Parliament the lawmaking part of the British government. Members of Parliament meet in London, England.

"If taxes are laid upon us . . . without our having a legal Representation . . . are we not reduced from . . . free Subjects to the miserable State of . . . slaves?"

Samuel Adams

had already given money and manpower for the French and Indian War.

King George did not listen. A year later, Parliament passed the Stamp Act. This act taxed the colonists on things made in America. Goods such as newspapers, insurance policies, deeds, mortgages, certificates, and even playing cards all required a stamp. Boston lawyer James Otis declared, "Taxation without representation is tyranny!"

James Otis and Samuel Adams were leaders of the patriots. These were colonists who wanted America to be free of British tyranny. About one-third of the colonists sided with the patriots. Another third, the Loyalists, remained loyal to King George. The last third was undecided.

During the summer of 1765, Boston patriots joined together to fight the Stamp Act. They became known as the Sons of Liberty. John Hancock, Paul Revere, Samuel Adams, and Sam's cousin, John Adams, were well-known Sons. Before long, Sons of Liberty groups sprang up throughout the colonies.

The Boston Sons of Liberty met secretly. They wrote articles for the *Boston Gazette* and other newspapers. They wrote pamphlets. They printed information on large sheets of paper called broadsides. They posted the broadsides on trees and buildings to tell people about the harsh British laws.

The Sons also organized a type of protest called a boycott. Merchants were urged to stop buying and selling British goods. The Sons even threatened stamp agents, insisting they quit selling stamps. "Stamp men" who would not quit might be tarred and feathered—covered with hot tar and bird feathers!

> a refusal to buy certain things from or deal with certain people or organizations

By the 1760s, most towns had a large tree called a Liberty Tree. Patriots gathered at the tree for meetings. One day some patriots strung up a dummy of a stamp agent named Andrew Oliver. It swung from Boston's Liberty Tree. A note was pinned to the dummy. It read, "What greater joy did New England see/Than a stamp man hanging on a tree." Oliver quit his job the next day.

Not long after this incident, a mob of angry colonists broke into the mansion of Thomas Hutchinson, the governor of the Massachusetts colony. They smashed windows and furniture. They threw his

WHY DID SOME COLONISTS TAR AND FEATHER?

Some colonists wanted British officials to quit their jobs. They tarred and feathered them to make them resign. The practice was cruel and painful. The mob brushed hot tar onto the official's skin or clothes. Then they threw pillow feathers onto the sticky tar. The angry mob would sometimes set their victim on a fence rail (a large log) and carry him out of town.

Bostonians protest the Stamp Act by burning stamps in a bonfire. German artist Daniel Chodowiecki created this print in 1784.

papers into the street. To the colonists, the governor represented British power.

In October 1765, a group of patriots met in New York for a Stamp Act Congress. Twenty-seven representatives from nine of the thirteen colonies were at this meeting. They drew up a declaration of colonial rights. They asked Parliament to repeal, or cancel, the Stamp Act.

King George heard about the protests in America. The Stamp Act was repealed in 1766. Bostonians celebrated with a grand party and fireworks on Boston Common, a large public park in central Boston. Little did they know of King George's next surprise.

NEXT QUESTION

WHAT INCIDENT IN BOSTON COST THE LIVES OF FIVE PEOPLE AND PUSHED THE COLONISTS CLOSER TO REBELLION?

Wealthy colonial men and women enjoy a cup of tea in the afternoon. Tea was one of the most popular beverages in colonial America.

TWO REDCOATS IN BOSTON

The people of Boston loved to drink tea. Many Bostonians drank at least two cups every day. In 1767 tea ranked fourth among America's imports from Britain. Only cotton and woolen cloth, linens, and ironware were more in demand in the colonies.

In the summer of 1767, the British government tried to tax the colonies again. Lawmakers passed the Townshend Acts. These laws placed an import duty of three pence (pennies) per pound on tea. Paper, glass, lead, and paint were also taxed. The money raised would pay the salaries of British soldiers. It would also pay for judges, governors, and customs officials. (Customs officials were men who collected taxes on goods entering the colonies.) This meant that colonial officials would then work for the king, not for the colonists.

More unfair laws! More taxes! The colonists were outraged. Samuel Adams and John Dickinson, a Pennsylvania lawyer, wrote articles and letters urging colonists to boycott British goods. Merchants up and down the East Coast signed boycott agreements. They agreed to stop importing goods from Britain. Merchants who refused to sign were labeled enemies of the people.

Colonial women joined in the boycott movement. They formed groups called the Daughters of Liberty. Instead of buying British imports, they made what they needed at home. They made tea from flowers and native plants, such as chamomile, raspberry, sassafras, and thyme.

This is the first of twelve letters John Dickinson wrote encouraging a boycott of British imports.

Colonial women used spinning wheels like this to spin yarn from wool. Colonists began making as much as they could at home to avoid buying taxed British imports.

Working in their homes, colonial women spun their own yarn and wove it into cloth. They used this homespun cloth to sew clothing for their families. To avoid buying British paint, many families lived in unpainted houses. British law stated that the colonies should trade only with Great Britain. But for years, some colonists had been smuggling goods from other countries. Colonists bought the smuggled goods because they did not have to pay import duties on them. After the Townshend Acts, smugglers grew more active. During the 1760s, for example, three-fourths of the tea drunk by Americans was smuggled from countries such as Holland.

smuggling — bringing goods into or out of a country illegally

Samuel Adams wrote a letter that made its way through the thirteen colonies. He claimed that taxes were taking away the colonists' rights guaranteed by British law. The law stated that no one could be taxed without agreeing to it. Adams asked all thirteen colonies to join Massachusetts in fighting for their rights. Colonists listened. They began to unite against the iron-fisted control of King George III.

After British customs officers were attacked, Parliament decided that Boston's rebels had gone too far. King George sent two warships to Boston along with two regiments of soldiers. (A regiment is a group of about five hundred to one thousand soldiers.)

Paul Revere made this print of British warships lining up in Boston Harbor in 1768. British soldiers were sent to Boston to keep angry colonists from disrupting trade.

Colonial boys make fun of a British soldier in Boston.

The soldiers marched through the streets, flashing their weapons. The soldiers wore bright red uniforms. As a result, colonists called them redcoats or lobsterbacks.

Bostonians were angry that British soldiers patrolled their streets. As for the soldiers, they would rather have been home in Britain. Bored with daily marches, the soldiers amused themselves by heckling and pestering the citizens. Sometimes on Sunday mornings, soldiers stood outside church doors and sang "Yankee Doodle" to mock the churchgoers.

a traditional song. British soldiers used the song to make fun of American colonists. But later, colonists adopted it as a patriotic theme.

On March 5, 1770, tempers reached the boiling point. A young man named Edward Garrick was walking by the Custom House, a government building in Boston. He spied a British officer he knew and began taunting him. Another soldier standing guard at the Custom House poked Garrick with his musket (a type of gun).

COLONIAL
BOSTON

CHARLES RIVER

MILL
POND

GREEN DRAGON
TAVERN

FANEUIL
HALL

CUSTOM
HOUSE

LONG WHARF

BOSTON
MASSACRE
SITE

BOSTON
COMMON

OLD SOUTH
MEETING
HOUSE

FORT HILL

GRIFFIN'S WHARF

BOSTON
HARBOR

An angry crowd gathered behind Garrick, including a former slave named Crispus Attucks. Snowballs and ice chunks began to fly. The guard called for more soldiers. The crowd quickly grew to more than four hundred. Some dared the soldiers to fire their weapons. "Lobsterbacks!" they shouted. "Cowards!"

WHO WAS PAUL REVERE?

Paul Revere was a silversmith—someone who makes dishes, jewelry, and other objects out of silver. He was also an engraver. Engraving is a way of printing pictures for books and newspapers. In 1770 he engraved a picture of the Boston Massacre. His picture showed the British soldiers mercilessly shooting innocent civilians. When Bostonians saw the picture, they grew angrier. Why should they pay taxes to support an army that was shooting American colonists?

One soldier, confused by all the noise, fired his gun. More shots followed. Crispus Attucks and two others fell dead. Two more died a short time later. The event became known as the Boston Massacre.

An angry Samuel Adams insisted that the British troops leave Boston at once. Governor Hutchinson knew there would be more trouble if the troops stayed.

Engrav'd Printed & Sold by Paul Revere Boston

This print by Paul Revere shows the Boston Massacre from a colonial point of view. It shows British soldiers firing at once on the colonists. The print doesn't show the mob that cornered and outnumbered the soldiers. Also, African American Crispus Attucks (on ground with head wound) is portrayed as a white colonist.

He reluctantly ordered the soldiers to Castle William, an island fort 2 miles (3 kilometers) away in Boston Harbor.

A month after the Boston Massacre, Parliament repealed the Townshend Acts. But the three-pence tax on tea was kept in force just to remind the colonists that Parliament still held power to tax them. Anger smoldered among the colonists because of the one remaining tax.

WHO WAS JOHN ADAMS?

John Adams was a young lawyer in Boston when the massacre took place. At trial he defended the soldiers who had killed the colonists. Adams personally sided with the patriots. But he believed that the soldiers had a right to a fair trial. The court dropped the charges against all but two of the men. Adams feared his career might come to an end after he defended the king's soldiers. Actually, his career was only beginning. He became a successful politician. Twenty-three years after the Boston massacre, he was elected the second president of the United States.

NEXT QUESTION

One patriot stirred the colonists to rebellion unlike any other.

WHO WAS GIVEN THE TITLE THE FATHER OF THE AMERICAN REVOLUTION?

WHO
WHAT
WHERE
WHY
WHEN
HOW
WHO
WHAT
WHERE
WHY
WHEN
HOW
WHO
WHAT
WHERE
HOW

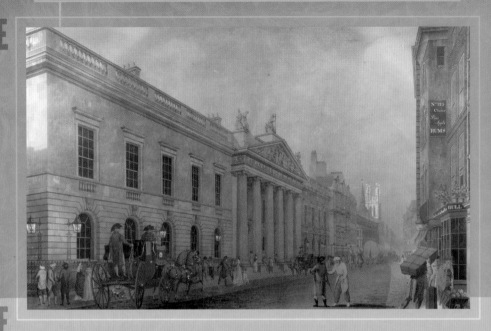

Thomas Malton (1726–1801) painted this view of the British East India Company's headquarters in London. The company sold Chinese and Indian tea in Great Britain and other countries.

THREE TEA AND TAXATION

After the Boston Massacre, Samuel Adams worked hard to keep alive the antitax movement. In 1772 he organized twenty-one patriots into a committee. The committee wrote letters and articles for newspapers. They sent the letters from colony to colony, spreading information. The committee reminded the colonists that their freedoms were being lost because of Britain's unfair tax laws. Within a few months, patriots started eighty committees in Massachusetts and other colonies.

Sam Adams believed that the colonies should be free of British rule. He wrote, "The country shall be independent,

governed by itself and not controlled by others

and we will be satisfied with nothing short of it." His powerful words influenced many people. Because of his dedication to the fight for American independence, he became known as the Father of the American Revolution.

Then came the pivotal year of 1773. British merchants were grumbling because Americans were buying more from smugglers and less from them. One company, the British East India Company, had nearly run out of money. Trade was so slow that the company had 18 million pounds (8 million kilograms) of tea piled up in its London warehouse.

To help the East India Company sell more tea, Parliament passed the Tea Act on May 10, 1773. The company shipped its tea from China and India to Great Britain and then to other countries. The Tea Act would allow the company to skip paying duties in Britain. By saving that money, the East India Company could sell tea at a lower price in the American colonies.

> "The country shall be independent, and we will be satisfied with nothing short of it."
> —Samuel Adams

WHO WAS SAMUEL ADAMS?

Sam Adams was so poor that his friends had to buy him new clothes for an important meeting. His hands trembled with palsy, a medical condition that causes uncontrollable shaking. But when Adams spoke, people listened. He was highly respected in Boston and very well liked.

Adams was descended from the Puritans who founded the Massachusetts Bay Colony. He knew how they had struggled to come to America to find freedom for themselves and their descendants. Adams was determined that Great Britain would not take away the hard-earned rights of his ancestors.

This print, which originally ran in the *Illustrated London News* in 1867, shows tea from India being loaded and unloaded on a London dock.

A special group of colonial merchants called agents were chosen to receive and sell the tea. These agents were known to be loyal to King George. They were the only merchants who could import the low-priced British tea. That gave them a monopoly of the trade. Other American tea merchants, as well as smugglers, would likely be put out of business. And of course, colonists would still have to pay a tax when tea shipments arrived in America.

monopoly complete control by one group over the buying and selling of something

An angry cry rose up from the colonists. What if Britain gave monopolies to other products? That would put more Americans out of business. What if Britain placed a tax on other goods? What if the tax on tea was raised? A patriot wrote an article for the *Boston Gazette*. It read, "If Parliament can of right tax us 10 pounds [a unit of British money] for any purpose, they may of right tax us 10,000, and so on, without end."

Parliament ignored the protests. In September 1773, seven ships sailed for the American colonies. They were loaded with two thousand

wooden chests containing almost 600,000 pounds (272,000 kg) of tea. Four of the ships, the *Dartmouth*, the *Eleanor*, the *Beaver*, and the *William*, headed for Boston. The other three sailed to New York; Philadelphia; and Charleston, South Carolina.

A replica of the *Beaver* sits in Boston Harbor.

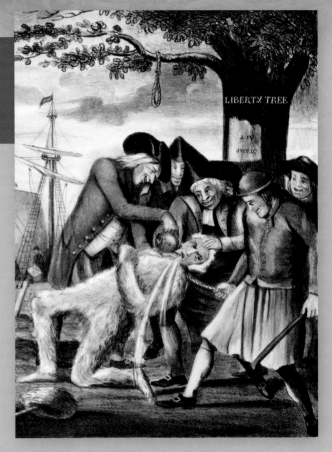

If the handpicked merchants paid the import taxes, the entire antitax movement would break apart. Patriots up and down the coast tried to force the merchants to quit their jobs. They threatened them with tarring and feathering if they accepted the tea and paid duties. The threats worked. By November every agent in New York, Philadelphia, and Charleston had quit.

But the Boston agents were a stubborn group. They refused to quit. Governor Hutchinson, who lived in Boston, had money invested in the East India Company. His sons, Elisha and Thomas, were two of the selected tea agents. Other agents were also relatives of the governor. Altogether, there were seven Boston agents eager to make a lot of money selling tea.

On November 2, the Boston committee delivered an official letter to two of the agents at two in the morning. The letter ordered the agents to appear at the Liberty Tree the following Wednesday. At exactly noon on that day, they were expected to quit their jobs. The letter ended with a warning—"Fail not upon your peril."

The other tea agents soon received the same threatening notice to quit their jobs. On Wednesday at noon, more than five hundred people crowded around the Liberty Tree. They waited, but the tea agents never showed up. Instead, they hid in a warehouse, unwilling to give up their jobs.

Over the next few weeks, the patriots held several meetings at Faneuil Hall. Led by Samuel Adams and John Hancock, they agreed that the tea agents should quit. Next, they voted that the tea ships should take the tea back to Great Britain.

a building in central Boston used as a marketplace and meeting hall

On November 28, 1773, the *Dartmouth* arrived in Boston Harbor. It carried 114 chests of tea.

TRADESMEN'S PROTEST AGAINST THE PROCEEDINGS OF THE MERCHANTS.

A broadside printed in November 1773 reports that tea agents were refusing to give in to protesters' demands.

If the tea was unloaded, duties would have to be paid. The Sons of Liberty printed broadsides and posted them to trees. The broadsides warned:

"FRIENDS! BRETHREN! COUNTRYMEN! That worst of plagues, the detested TEA, shipped for this Port by the East–India Company, is now arrived in this Harbour."

The broadsides alerted the colonists that they should meet at Faneuil Hall that very day. They should refuse to pay the tea tax and should unite against British tyranny.

The next day, more than six thousand people flocked to Faneuil Hall. The crowd was so large that the group moved to the Old South Meeting House, the biggest building in Boston. At the meeting, the patriots agreed that the three ships should return to Britain. Twenty-five men with muskets

Faneuil Hall, shown in this 1776 print, served as a meeting place for large public gatherings.

The Old South Meeting House in Boston is one of the sixteen sites on a 2.5-mile (4 km) historical walking tour called the Freedom Trail.

were chosen to board the ships and guard the cargo. They were to make sure no one unloaded the tea. Meanwhile, many of the Loyalist tea agents fled to the safety of Castle William. They were afraid of being tarred and feathered. Tensions in Boston were mounting. What would happen next?

NEXT QUESTION

WHERE IN BOSTON DID THE TEA PARTY ACTUALLY TAKE PLACE?

WHO
WHAT
WHERE
WHY
WHEN
HOW
WHO
WHAT
WHERE
WHY
WHEN
HOW
WHO
WHAT
WHERE
WHY
WHEN
HOW

The *Dartmouth* can be seen in Boston Harbor in this print.

FOUR SALTWATER TEA

The *Dartmouth* moved from Boston's Long Wharf to Griffin's Wharf, southeast of the city. It was soon joined by the *Eleanor* and the *Beaver*. The fourth ship, the *William*, had wrecked off the coast of Cape Cod. (The ships bound for New York and Philadelphia never delivered their tea cargoes. Tea sent to South Carolina ended up rotting in a warehouse.)

The law stated that the captain of the *Dartmouth* had only twenty days to unload his cargo. The cargo had to be unloaded and all taxes paid by midnight on December 16, 1773. After that, customs officials could seize the cargo and sell it.

Governor Hutchinson was determined that the tea would be unloaded and the taxes paid. To make sure no ships left Boston, he ordered two warships to block the harbor. Their heavy guns were aimed at Griffin's Wharf. Hutchinson also ordered soldiers on Castle William to load one hundred cannons and have them ready to fire.

Again, the Sons of Liberty asked the tea agents to quit. Again, they refused. The Sons asked customs officials to allow the ships to return to Britain with the tea. Permission was denied.

In the days leading to December 16, the Sons of Liberty met in secret behind closed doors. They finally reached a decision. The only way to keep from paying taxes on the tea was to destroy it. Plans for the "tea party" were set in motion.

The morning of December 16 dawned cold and rainy. Excitement ran high as about seven thousand people crowded into the Old South Meeting House.

Colonists attended a rowdy meeting at the Old South Meeting House. French painter C. J. Hoffbauer (1875–1906) captured this scene.

Francis Rotch, part owner of the *Dartmouth*, attended the meeting. The patriots ordered him to ask Governor Hutchinson for permission to return his ship to Britain. Rotch rode to Milton, 8 miles (13 km) away, to meet with the governor.

At quarter to six in the evening, he finally returned to the Old South Meeting House. The crowd of anxious colonists waited for the governor's answer. Rotch told the crowd that the governor would not allow any tea ship to leave until all taxes were paid.

The patriots were furious. "Who knows how tea will mingle with sea water?" someone yelled. The crowd cheered. "A mob! A mob!"

Many patriots had already guessed how the meeting would end. More than fifty men had spent the afternoon disguising themselves as Mohawks. They did not want soldiers or officials to recognize them. They covered their faces with soot, grease, or paint. They draped blankets over their shoulders and pulled on woolen caps. At the meeting, they stood near the doorway.

Native American people originally from modern-day New York State and Canada

Sam Adams stepped to the front of the room. "This meeting can do nothing more to save the country," he announced. Those words were a signal for the tea party to begin. A loud whoop went up from the "Indians."

"The Mohawks are here!" someone shouted.

"Hurrah for Griffin's Wharf!"

"Boston Harbor [is] a teapot tonight."

"Let every man do what is right in his own eyes," called John Hancock as the meeting broke up.

The protesters gripped axes that looked like tomahawks. They marched down Milk and Hutchinson streets to Griffin's Wharf. As they approached the three tea ships, more patriots joined them. They grew quiet when they reached the ships. They did not want to draw attention from the British warships.

At the wharf, the men split into three groups and boarded the ships. They ordered the crews to open the cargo areas. The men lifted the 320-pound (145 kg) wooden tea chests to the deck with pulleys and ropes. They slashed the chests open with their axes, sliced through tough canvas bags, and dumped the tea leaves overboard.

Crowds watch as colonists dressed as Native Americans dump British tea overboard on December 16, 1773. This engraving was created in the mid-1800s.

Since the tide was out, the water was only a few feet deep. The tea began to pile up around the ship railings. Some men stayed below in the harbor to stir the tea into the water and smash any remaining chests. (Only two tea chests remain of the original 342.)

A crowd lined Griffin's Wharf, watching the action by moonlight. The guns from the warships never fired. Admiral John Montagu, commander of the British navy, was afraid of hurting innocent bystanders. He did not want another incident like the Boston Massacre. The guns were silent. The crowd was silent. The only sounds were axes splitting wood and chests hitting water.

The patriots wanted every bit of tea destroyed. They caught one man hiding tea inside his coat lining. The man's coat was torn off as he struggled to get away. When another man was found stealing tea, his tea was flung into the muddy water along with his hat and fancy wig.

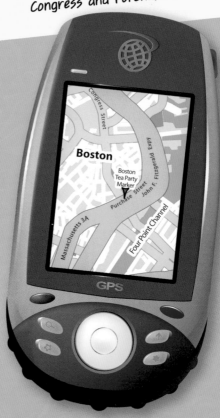

WHERE IS THE HISTORICAL MARKER FOR THE BOSTON TEA PARTY?
Boston has changed a lot since colonial days. Griffin's Wharf no longer exists. But a plaque set in stone marks the official site of the tea party. The marker is at the intersection of Congress and Purchase streets.

By nine at night, the patriots had dumped all the tea overboard. They took off their shoes and shook out any remaining leaves. They swept the decks clean so no tea would remain. Not a thing had been damaged, except, of course, the tea. Also, one brass padlock had accidentally been broken. It was carefully replaced the next day with a new one.

Two by two, the men left the ships, carrying their axes over their shoulders. They were exhausted. Joshua Wyeth, a participant, would later say, "I never worked harder in my life." One patriot pulled out a fife (a musical instrument). He played "Yankee Doodle" as they made their way through the crowd.

Admiral Montagu had watched everything from a nearby house. He opened a window and yelled, "Well, boys, you've had a fine, pleasant evening for your Indian caper, haven't you? But mind, you've got to pay the fiddler yet!" He was right. The patriots would pay a price for their "caper."

NEXT QUESTION

The tea party at Griffin's Wharf was the spark that ignited the Revolutionary War.

HOW LONG DID IT TAKE FROM THE TEA PARTY OF 1773 UNTIL THE FIRST SHOTS OF WAR WERE FIRED?

WHO
WHAT
WHERE
WHY
WHEN
HOW
WHO
WHAT
WHERE
WHY
WHEN
HOW
WHO
WHAT
WHERE
WHY
WHEN
HOW

The Green Dragon Tavern was a popular meeting place in Boston. This print is from 1773.

FIVE PAYING THE FIDDLER

The morning after the tea party, Sam Adams wrote a letter describing the event. Paul Revere carried the letter by horseback from Boston to New York. It was December 17, 1773.

From New York, the news spread fast to Philadelphia and throughout the thirteen colonies. Church bells rang and colonists cheered when they heard of the bold stand Bostonians had taken against the king of Great Britain.

Soon a new song was heard in Boston's Green Dragon Tavern, a popular spot for patriot meetings. The song went, "Rally, Mohawks! Bring out your axes/And tell King

George, we'll pay no taxes!"

Just before Christmas, Sam Adams wrote a letter to a friend in London saying, "You cannot imagine the height of joy that sparkles in the eyes and animates the countenances [faces] as well as the hearts of all we meet on this occasion."

Sam's cousin, John, wrote in his diary, "There is a Dignity, a Majesty . . . in this last Effort of the Patriots that I greatly admire. . . . This Destruction of the Tea is so bold, so daring, so firm . . . and it must have so important Consequences and so lasting, that I cannot but consider it as an Epocha [unique period] in History."

Christmas came and went. The children played in the snow. They rode their sleds down the slopes of Boston Common. People went about their business, wondering what would happen when King George heard about the destruction of the tea. The following spring they found out.

The king was furious. In modern terms, those 342 chests of tea were worth about one million dollars. Their destruction was high treason. The leaders of such a criminal act were to be arrested, if not hanged. One Parliament member insisted, "The town of Boston must be knocked down about their ears and destroyed."

> "Rally, Mohawks!
> Bring out your axes
> And tell King George
> we'll pay no taxes!"
> —celebration song popular
> after the Boston Tea Party

the crime of trying to overthrow one's own government

The king decided to make Boston an example for the other colonies. In 1774 Parliament passed a series of acts called the Coercive Acts. To coerce means to force someone to behave a certain way. The acts were aimed at forcing Boston's rebels to obey British law. King George thought that punishing Boston would make the other colonies tremble with fear.

The colonists called them the Intolerable (that is, impossible to put up with) Acts. The acts closed the port of Boston to both foreign and coastal shipping. The port would stay closed until the colonists paid for the destroyed tea and the tax on it. The capital of the Massachusetts Colony moved from Boston to Salem.

The acts canceled the charter of Massachusetts. That took away the colony's freedom to govern itself. The members of the Massachusetts Council (high court) were to be appointed by the king, not chosen by the colonists. Town meetings were no longer allowed unless the governor gave his permission.

A 1774 broadside announces an act to block Boston Harbor. Closing the harbor was one of the Coercive Acts put in place by King George to force Boston to obey British law.

To add to Boston's troubles, King George sent thousands of soldiers and four more warships to Boston. A British military leader, General Thomas Gage, replaced Hutchinson as the governor of Massachusetts.

On June 1, 1774, Parliament ordered the port of Boston officially closed. Ships sat idle. Stores were shut, and people were out of work. Bostonians were faced with many shortages. Would they pay the tax, or would they starve?

King George was in for a surprise. Colonists from Maine to Georgia rallied to Boston's aid. They sent shipments of food, cattle, sheep, corn, wheat, rice, and money to Boston. The tea party and the resulting punishment of the city united the thirteen colonies as nothing else had. "An attack on one of our sister colonies, to compel submission to arbitrary [unfair] taxes, is an attack made on all British America," announced Thomas Jefferson of Virginia. Patriotism swept like fire across the colonies.

"An attack on one of our sister colonies, to compel submission to arbitrary [unfair] taxes, is an attack made on all British America."

Thomas Jefferson

The First Continental Congress, shown in this painting based on the work of British artist Robert Edge Pine (ca. 1720–1788), took place in 1774 in Philadelphia.

Patriots from Virginia, including Jefferson and Patrick Henry, called for a meeting of representatives from all the colonies. They wanted to discuss their complaints against King George III. On September 5, 1774, the First Continental Congress met in Carpenters' Hall in Philadelphia. The delegates decided to boycott all trade with Britain until it repealed the Intolerable Acts.

The Intolerable Acts, however, were not repealed. Instead, more soldiers came from Great Britain. Colonial militia began to march and drill in open fields. The patriots swore they would never fire the first shot. But what if the redcoats fired at them? They wanted to be ready. The patriots began making

ordinary citizens who join together to fight as soldiers

muskets. They began to store ammunition (things that can be fired from weapons) in towns such as Concord, near Boston.

General Gage grew nervous. He feared an uprising of the colonists. It was time for a show of force by the powerful British army. First, Gage sent soldiers to Lexington, another town near Boston. The soldiers had orders to arrest Sam Adams and John Hancock. Those two troublemakers had to be stopped, once and for all. Next, the soldiers were ordered to seize the colonists' ammunition in Concord.

The Sons of Liberty learned about the soldiers' march toward Lexington. On the evening of April 18, 1775, they sent Paul Revere, William Dawes, and Samuel Prescott to warn Adams and Hancock. The messengers sped to Lexington, alerting patriots along the way. Early the next morning, about seventy colonists faced about seven hundred redcoats in an open area called Lexington Green.

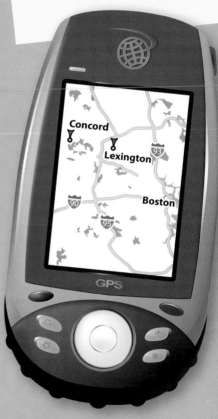

WHERE ARE LEXINGTON AND CONCORD?
Lexington is about 12 miles (19 km) northwest of Boston. Concord is 7 miles (12 km) west of Lexington.

Paul Revere made his famous ride through the roads of Massachusetts to alert colonists that British troops were heading toward Lexington.

A British officer ordered the large group to break up and leave the green.

Suddenly, a gunshot shattered the morning calm. More gunfire followed. Eight patriots died, and nine were wounded. One British soldier was wounded. No one knows who fired that first shot. But it came to be called the shot heard 'round the world. The conflict on Lexington Green was the first battle of the American Revolution. That same day, colonists and British soldiers fought in the Battle of Concord.

The Battles of Lexington and Concord took place sixteen months after the Boston Tea Party. The defiant act of the tea dumpers and the resulting anger of the British government led to the deadly clash between Britain and its colonies.

The Revolutionary War lasted more than seven years. The patriots' victory in 1783 brought independence to the American colonies. And it gave birth to a new nation, the United States of America.

WHAT HAPPENED AT THE BATTLE OF CONCORD?

After the Battle of Lexington, the British soldiers marched on to Concord. They destroyed a small amount of ammunition and weapons. But the colonists had hidden most of it.

By midday hundreds of patriots made their way to Concord to fight the British. As the redcoats marched back to Boston, the Americans shot at them from behind trees, walls, and houses.

A total of 73 British soldiers were killed, and 174 were wounded. Forty-nine colonists were killed, and 39 were wounded. It was a surprise victory for the American patriots against the mighty British army.

NEXT QUESTION

HOW DO WE KNOW SO MUCH ABOUT THE BOSTON TEA PARTY?

Primary Source: John Andrews's Letter

The best way to see into the past and learn about any historical event is with primary sources. Primary sources are created near the time being studied. They include diaries, letters, newspaper articles, documents, speeches, personal papers, pamphlets, photos, paintings, and other items. They are made by people who have direct, firsthand knowledge of the event.

We know about the Boston Tea Party because of the wealth of primary source material available. One example is John Andrews's eyewitness account of the march of the tea party protesters from the Old South Meeting House. Andrews was a Boston merchant. Two days after the tea party, on December 18, 1773, he wrote to William Barrell, a merchant in Philadelphia. Here is a portion of the letter:

> Shouts were made that [led] me, while drinking tea at home, to go out and know the cause of it. The [meeting] house was so crowded I could get no farther than the porch, when I found the moderator was just declaring the meeting to be dissolved, which caused another general shout, outdoors and in, and three cheers. . . . They say the actors were Indians from Narragansett . . . cloathed in blankets with the heads muffled, and copper-colored [faces], being each armed with a hatchet or axe, and pair [of] pistols.

To learn more about the Boston Tea Party, study other primary sources such as eighteenth-century maps of Boston Harbor, Governor Hutchinson's papers, Sam Adams's letters, John Adams's diary, newspaper articles, or the eyewitness account of tea party participant George Hewes.

TELL YOUR
BOSTON TEA PARTY STORY

Pretend it is 1773, and you are a member of the Sons of Liberty in Boston. Your job is to write a secret letter urging your friends to destroy the tea aboard the *Dartmouth*, the *Eleanor*, and the *Beaver*.

WHAT is your name?

WHY did you join the Sons of Liberty?

WHEN should your friends meet to join the Boston Tea Party?

WHERE should they meet?

WHAT are the dangers involved?

WHY must the tea be destroyed?

USE **WHO, WHAT, WHERE WHY, WHEN, AND HOW** TO THINK OF OTHER QUESTIONS TO HELP YOU CREATE YOUR STORY!

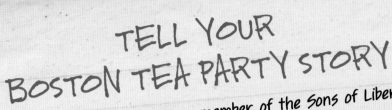

Timeline

1600s

Britain sets up permanent colonies in North America.

1763

The **French and Indian War** ends.

1764

The British parliament passes the Sugar Act.

1765

Parliament passes the Stamp Act.

Samuel Adams helps organize the Sons of Liberty.

Patriots meet in New York for a Stamp Act Congress.

1766

Britain repeals the Stamp Act.

1767

The Townshend Acts place taxes on lead, glass, paper, paint, and tea.

1768

British troops are sent to Boston.

1770

Five colonists die in the **Boston Massacre**.

Parliament repeals the Townshend Acts, except for the tea tax.

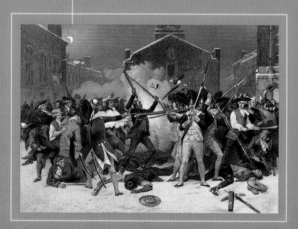

1772

Samuel Adams forms a committee in Boston. More committees follow throughout the colonies.

1773

Parliament passes the Tea Act.

In November three British tea ships arrive in Boston Harbor.

In December patriots dump 342 chests of tea into Boston Harbor.

King George puts a British military general, Thomas Gage, in charge of Massachusetts.

1774

Parliament passes the Coercive Acts (Intolerable Acts).

Parliament orders the closing of the port of Boston.

In September the First Continental Congress meets in Philadelphia.

1775

Paul Revere and others ride to Lexington to warn the patriots.

The American Revolution begins with the **Battle of Lexington**.

The Battle of Concord takes place.

Gage sends out an order to arrest patriots Samuel Adams and John Hancock.

1783

American colonists defeat the British army to win the American Revolution.

Source Notes

8   Theodore Draper, *A Struggle for Power: The American Revolution* (New York: Random House, 1996), 219.

8   Ibid.

9   Daniel A. Smith, T*ax Crusaders and the Politics of Direct Democracy* (New York: Routledge, 1998), 174 n.13.

10 A. J. Langguth, *Patriots: The Men Who Started the American Revolution* (New York: Simon and Schuster, 1988), 53.

20–21 Mark Puls, *Samuel Adams: Father of the American Revolution* (New York: Palgrave Macmillan, 2006), 78.

21 Ibid.

23 Wesley S. Griswold, *The Night the Revolution Began: The Boston Tea Party, 1773* (Brattleboro, VT: Stephen Greene Press, 1972), 18.

23 Ibid.

25 Francis S. Drake, *Tea Leaves: Being a Collection of Letters and Documents Relating to the Shipment of Tea to the American Colonies in the Year 1773 by the East India Tea Company* (Boston: A. O. Crane, 1884), 282.

26 Laurence Greene, *America Goes to Press: The News of Yesterday* (Indianapolis: Bobbs-Merrill, 1936), 17.

30 Griswold, *The Night the Revolution Began*, 91.

30 Langguth, *Patriots*, 179.

33 Drake, *Tea Leaves*, lxxii.

33 Griswold, *The Night the Revolution Began*, 1972), 105.

34–35 Langguth, *Patriots*, 184.

35 Ibid.

35 Puls, *Samuel Adams*, 147.

35 Benjamin Woods Labaree, *The Boston Tea Party* (Boston: Northeastern University Press, 1979), 145.

35 Griswold, *The Night the Revolution Began*, 120.

37 Thomas Fleming, *Liberty! The American Revolution* (New York: Viking, 1997), 87.

37 Ibid.

42 Henry Steele Commager and Richard B. Morris, eds., *The Spirit of 'Seventy-Six: The Story of the American Revolution as Told by Participants*. Vol. 1 (Indianapolis: Bobbs-Merrill, 1958), 4.

Selected Bibliography

Bennett, William J. *America: The Last Best Hope*. Vol. 1, *From the Age of Discovery to a World of War*. Nashville: Nelson Current, 2006.

Draper, Theodore. *A Struggle for Power: The American Revolution*. New York: Random House, 1996.

Fleming, Thomas. *Liberty! The American Revolution*. New York: Viking, 1997.

Langguth, A. J. *Patriots: The Men Who Started the American Revolution*. New York: Simon and Schuster, 1988.

Puls, Mark. *Samuel Adams: Father of the American Revolution*. New York: Palgrave Macmillan, 2006.

Further Reading and Websites

Amstel, Marsha. *Sybil Ludington's Midnight Ride*. Minneapolis: Millbrook Press, 2000. This illustrated book relates the true story of sixteen-year-old Sybil Luddington's ride to warn American soldiers of the advancing British troops in 1777.

The Boston Tea Party, 1773
http://www.eyewitnesstohistory.com/teaparty.htm
Read a Boston shoemaker's eyewitness account of the action that sparked the events leading to the American Revolution.

Boston Tea Party Historical Society
http://www.boston-tea-party.org/
Website visitors can compare eight different accounts of the Boston Tea Party, learn about the British point of view, and read biographies of tea party participants.

Figley, Marty Rhodes. *John Greenwood's Journey to Bunker Hill*. Minneapolis: Millbrook Press, 2011. Witness the Revolutionary War through the eyes of a fifteen-year-old colonial boy who joins the Revolutionary army as a fife player.

Herbert, Janis. *The American Revolution for Kids: A History with 21 Activities*. Chicago: Chicago Review Press, 2002. The Revolutionary War comes into focus as readers combine the history of the 1700s with hands-on activities.

Mattern, Joanne. *The Cost of Freedom: Crispus Attucks and the Boston Massacre*. New York: Rosen Publishing Group, 2004. This biography discusses Attucks's role in the fight for American independence.

Miller, Brandon. *Growing Up in Revolution and the New Nation, 1775 to 1800*. Minneapolis: Lerner Publications Company, 2003. Through diaries and letters, Miller looks at what life was like for young people in colonial America.

Roop, Peter, and Connie Roop. *The Top-Secret Adventure of John Darragh, Revolutionary War Spy*. Minneapolis: Graphic Universe, 2011. Based on true accounts, this graphic novel tells the story of a fourteen-year-old spy in Revolutionary War America.

Whitelaw, Nancy. *The Shot Heard Round the World: The Battles of Lexington and Concord*. Greensboro, NC: Morgan Reynolds, 2001. The story opens with the Boston Massacre and tells of events in Boston leading to the first battles of the Revolutionary War. Readers learn more about historical figures such as Sam Adams and John Hancock.

Index

Photo Acknowledgments

The images in this book are used with the permission of: © iStockphoto.com/DNY59, p. 1; © Aksen/Dreamstime.com, pp. 1 (background), and all tea leaves backgrounds; © iStockphoto.com/sx70, pp. 3 (top), 10, 18 (top), 19, 21, 41; © iStockphoto.com/Ayse Nazli Deliormanli, pp. 3 (bottom), 43 (bottom left); © iStockphoto.com/Serdar Yagci, pp. 4-5 (background), 43 (background); © Bill Hauser/Independent Picture Service, pp. 4-5 (map), 17, 32 (inset), 39 (inset); © iStockphoto.com/Andrey Pustovoy, pp. 4, 14, 23, 27; REUTERS/Brian Snyder , p. 4 (inset); © MPI/Hulton Archive/Getty Images, p. 5; © New York Public Library/Art Resource, NY, p. 6; © Image Asset Management Ltd./SuperStock, p. 7; The Granger Collection, New York, pp. 8, 11, 18 (bottom), 24, 26, 31; Courtesy of the Massachusetts Historical Society, pp. 9, 13, 25, 36; © North Wind Picture Archives, pp. 12, 16, 22, 40, 43 (bottom right); © Pat & Chuck Blackley/Alamy, p. 14 (inset); © The Bridgeman Art Library/Getty Images, p. 15; © British Library, London, Great Britain/HIP/Art Resource, NY, p. 20; © Kevin Fleming/CORBIS, p. 23 (inset); © Kim Karpeles/Alamy, p. 27 (inset); © 2d Alan King/Alamy, p. 28; © SuperStock/SuperStock, p. 29; © iStockphoto.com/Talshiar, pp. 32, 39; © Bettmann/CORBIS, pp. 34, 37; © H. Armstrong Roberts/ClassicStock/The Image Works, p. 38; The Art Archive/Culver Pictures, p. 44 (top); © Stock Montage/Hulton Archive/Getty Images, p. 44 (bottom); © Hulton Archive/Getty Images, p. 45.

Front cover: The Art Archive/Private Collection/Marc Charmet.
Back cover: © Aksen/Dreamstime.com (background).